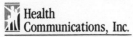

Other Books In This Series Are:

Where Do I Draw The Line?
Carla Wills-Brandon, M.A.

I Don't Need Therapy But . . .
Laurie Weiss, M.A.

Angry? Do You Mind If I Scream?
Devon Weber

Health Communications, Inc.
3201 S.W. 15th Street
Deerfield Beach, FL 33442-8190
Phone: (800) 851-9100

STRESSED OUT?

A Guidebook For Taking Care Of Yourself

Bryan E. Robinson, Ph.D.

Health Communications, Inc.
Deerfield Beach, Florida

Bryan E. Robinson, Ph.D.
University of North Carolina at Charlotte
Charlotte, North Carolina

© 1991 Bryan E. Robinson
ISBN 1-55874-142-9

Publisher: Health Communications, Inc.
            3201 S.W. 15th Street
            Deerfield Beach, Florida 33442-8190

1. ARE YOU ADDICTED TO STRESSFUL LIVING?

Do you rush around moaning about the shortage of time? Do you wail at the clock and shake your fist at the heavens because there's just not enough time to do everything? Is your life fast-paced and high-pressured without time for self-renewal, joy and serenity? If so, you could be addicted to stressful living, trying to cram 48 hours into 24.

Many of us are caught up in the frantic pace of today's world, speed-reading, quick-fixing, rush-houring, fast-tracking and hustling and bustling ourselves to death. Our relationships become brittle from neglect. On the job or in the home, addiction to fast-paced living has no boundaries — whether it's painting the house, shuffling the kids to and from school, preparing dinner or bringing work home from the office. Many of us try to do too much in too little time. If you are overworked and stressed out, if you are living your life for everyone but yourself, if you want to slow down but don't know how, this workbook is for you.

Overloaded schedules create stress. Stress causes the body to produce the hormone adrenaline, which has an effect similar to amphetamines or "speed." Fast-trackers often unknowingly put themselves under stress to get the body to pump an adrenaline fix. Addicted to the adrenaline rush, fast-trackers require larger doses to maintain the high that they create by putting themselves and those around them under stress. They thrive on stress by biting off more than they can chew, driving themselves beyond human endurance and pushing those around them to reach unrealistic deadlines.

OVER-INVESTMENT IN WORK

Fast-trackers and superachievers often satisfy their "busyholism" by over-investing in their jobs. Work becomes their drug of choice. They are as powerless over their work compulsions as alcoholics are over drinking. They get high from work, go on binges and get hangovers as they ultimately start to come down. The downward swing is accompanied by withdrawal, irritability, anxiety and depression. Over-investment at work can lead to burn-out and even death. It can destroy the family just like any other addiction.

What makes work abusive or addictive, as opposed to healthy or constructive, is the degree to which work interferes with physical health, personal happiness or intimate and social relationships. For adult children from dysfunctional homes, excessive work medicates emotional pain by making them feel better. They get hooked because work keeps them from having to deal with unpleasant feelings that they have stored in their bodies since childhood.

The irony of the disease is that work addicts suffer more problems on the job than their colleagues. Work addicts are generally not team players and often have difficulty cooperatively problem-solving, negotiating and compromising. Because they are over-invested in their work, they tend to suffer extreme stress and burn-out, and subsequently their efficiency declines.

In some ways overworking is harder to kick than the other addictions because it is the only one that draws applause. Compulsive work is accepted and encouraged at every level of our society. Amid praise, slaps on the back, fat paychecks and gold plaques, marriages break up, friendships dissolve, work effectiveness ebbs and health problems appear. No one, least of all the work addict, understands what went wrong. Work addicts drown their sorrows by rolling up their sleeves and immersing themselves deeper in their jobs.

— EXERCISE 1: ARE YOU OVERLY INVESTED IN WORK?

Here is a self-test to help you review the role work plays in your life. This test will help you determine if you or someone you know is over-invested in work. When you have responded to all 25 statements, add up the numbers in the blanks for your total score.

- 25 to 54 = Not overly invested.
- 55 to 69 = Mildly overly invested.
- 70 to 100 = Highly overly invested.

Read each of the 25 statements below and decide how much each one pertains to you. Use the following rating scale:

1 = *Never true*
2 = *Sometimes true*
3 = *Often true*
4 = *Always true*

Put the number that best fits you in the blank beside each statement.

_____ 1. I prefer to do most things myself rather than ask for help.

_____ 2. I get very impatient when I have to wait for someone else or when something takes too long, such as long slow-moving lines.

_____ 3. I seem to be in a hurry and racing against the clock.

_____ 4. I get irritated when I am interrupted while I am in the middle of something.

_____ 5. I stay busy and keep many "irons in the fire."

_____ 6. I find myself doing two or three things at one time, such as eating lunch and writing a memo, while talking on the telephone.

_____ 7. I over-commit myself by biting off more than I can chew.

_____ 8. I feel guilty when I am not working on something.

_____ 9. It is important that I see the concrete results of what I do.

_____ 10. I am more interested in the final result of my work than in the process.

_____ 11. Things just never seem to move fast enough or get done fast enough for me.

_____ 12. I lose my temper when things don't go my way or work out to suit me.

_____ 13. I ask the same question, without realizing it, after I've already been given the answer.

_____ 14. I spend a lot of time mentally planning and thinking about future events, while tuning out the here and now.

_____ 15. I find myself continuing to work after my co-workers have called it quits.

_____ 16. I get angry when people don't meet my standards of perfection.

_____ 17. I get upset when I am in situations where I cannot be in control.

_____ 18. I tend to put myself under pressure with self-imposed deadlines.

_____ 19. It is hard for me to relax when I'm not working.

_____ 20. I spend more time working than socializing with friends, on hobbies or on leisure activities.

_____ 21. I dive into projects to get a head start before all the phases have been finalized.

_____ 22. I get upset with myself for making even the smallest mistake.

_____ 23. I put more thought, time and energy into my work than I do into my relationships with my spouse (or lover) and family.

_____ 24. I forget, ignore or minimize important family celebrations such as birthdays, reunions, anniversaries or holidays.

_____ 25. I make important decisions before I have all the facts and have
a chance to think them through
thoroughly.

STRESS ADDICTION ON THE FAST TRACK

The following 10 signs are associated with
stress addiction. Fast-trackers are usually in
a hurry, have a strong need to control, are
perfectionists, have difficulty in relationships, binge on work, have difficulty relaxing and having fun, experience brownouts,
are impatient and irritable, feel inadequate
and are self-neglectful.

1. HURRYING AND STAYING BUSY

Things never move fast enough for me.
That's why I'm always doing three or four
things at a time. There have been times when
I've asked my secretary to do something, and
if she hasn't done it in the next 60 seconds, I
have to catch myself because I think, "Why
hasn't she gone to do that?" Then I have to tell
myself, "If you want it done immediately, you
have to tell her that, and you don't need it
immediately." Just because it's on my agenda
and it's my issue doesn't mean it's hers or

someone else's. It's not that I get mad at her, I just think, "But why isn't she doing it?" Or I think about my supervisor and think I need to light a fire under him. "Why doesn't he see this as a priority?" Somehow I think if I dive in and do it my way, I'll do it better.

Nothing ever moves fast enough for stress addicts. They are haunted by a constant sense of urgency and are always struggling against the limits of time:

As I go out the door at home ready to leave, I think I'd better feed the cat or take something out of the freezer. I just try to cram in one more thing. I look at my watch and realize I have 10 minutes, so I'll put a load of clothes in the washer. While I'm in the basement, I'll pick up something and put it up. Before I know it, 15 minutes have passed and I end up being late.

Unless many things are going at once, fast-trackers are discontented. They usually have so many things to do there are not enough hours in the day to finish them. Staying busy and keeping many irons in the fire become important ends in themselves. Conducting two or three activities at once is usual behavior. The faster stress addicts can bathe, eat, get the kids to day care or clean the house, the more time they have for additional work and the better they feel:

> I'll be talking to someone on the phone, filing my nails and thinking about what I'll wear to work the next day. I've read magazines at stoplights or studied for a test, drunk coffee and eaten breakfast while driving.

Saving time is important in everything they do. Stress addicts take short cuts wherever possible, sometimes even when it sacrifices the quality of work. The more work they can produce, the better they feel. A writer told his friend that he had signed five different book contracts. His friend looked at him in dismay and said, "You need to check yourself into a mental hospital!"

"Don't worry," the writer reassured him. "They're not all due on the same day."

The friend thought the writer's behavior was strange. The writer thought his friend's reaction was silly. He was addicted to work and didn't know it.

EXERCISE 2: HOW CAN YOU SLOW DOWN?

Think about some ways you can slow down the pulse and rhythm of your daily life. For example, set aside a period of time to deliberately eat slower, talk slower, walk slower and drive slower. Slowing down might mean saying no when you are already over-committed. In the workplace it could mean not putting yourself under unrealistic deadlines or putting self-imposed time limits on important things that must get done. It might mean listing priorities and eliminating the less important items on your list. Or it could mean giving yourself extra time to get where you need to go and building time cushions into your schedule so that you have time to have a casual conversation with a colleague or friend. The examples are endless and the strategies we take are different because our lives and jobs are so varied.

In the space below write down as many ways as you can think of to slow down at work, at home and at play. Keep adding to this list as new ideas come to you later on. Then put these ideas into action slowly, one by one and one step at a time.

▬ EXERCISE 3: SLOW DOWN WITH MEDITATION

One of the best ways to slow down and achieve serenity is through meditation. There are many types of meditation: prayer, inspirational readings, relaxation exercises, quiet reflection, yoga or what I call deep meditation. This deep meditation exercise is designed to help you slow down on your own:

DEEP MEDITATION

In a quiet and comfortable place, close your eyes and get comfortable. Clear your mind of cluttered thoughts and focus on your breathing. Inhale and exhale a few times. Let your body become completely relaxed from head to toe. Continue breathing and relaxing until you are in a totally relaxed state.

When you are relaxed, visualize yourself going through your day at a slow pace. Go through your daily routine from the time you get out of bed until the time you go to sleep that night. See yourself getting out of bed, having breakfast, getting dressed and going to work.

Now see yourself at your workplace. Take yourself through your daily routine, all the while slowing yourself down. See yourself eating slower, talking slower, walking slower, driving slower and doing one thing at a time. See the events of the day happening vividly and imagine the smallest details of each one. Let any images of you hurrying pass by. Notice how you begin to feel as your routine slows down. How do others around you feel?

Conclude your meditation by imaging going to bed that night. How do you feel as you go to bed and drift off to sleep? Don't be discouraged if initially you feel discomfort or even anxiety. Remember, you're changing a habit that you have had for a long time. Slowing down takes time, practice and patience.

Continue this exercise as often as you feel the need. Each time you complete this meditation, write your feelings and thoughts below. Notice how your feelings begin to change with practice and you feel more comfortable with your slower pace.

2. *NEED TO CONTROL*

Fast-trackers and stress addicts have an obsessive need to control themselves and everything in their lives. They cannot and will not ask for help, preferring to do things themselves rather than share the workload. Many employers who are addicted to stress do not want to give up control of situations, so they refuse to delegate authority to employees because no one else can do what needs to be done as fast or as well as they can. Employers who do everything themselves get to maintain more control over the situation rather than handing the controls over to someone else.

Stress addicts often get upset in situations where they cannot be in control or when things do not go their way. Being a part of group decision-making where negotiation and compromise ensure that everyone's voice is heard, such as committee work, civic groups or a group of friends deciding on a restaurant, challenges the stress addict's need to control. As a result they are overworked, tired and overstressed. They often put co-workers in a double bind by denying them an opportunity to carry their share of workloads, and then resenting and complaining that they have to do it all themselves.

I found it interesting to watch a colleague who insisted on doing all the planning for an annual conference of which he was chairperson. When other committee members volunteered to help, he ignored their offers. Once he became overloaded, he vented his anger toward the other members, charging that they sat back while he did all the work. The inability or unwillingness to ask for help assures quantity control but not quality control.

Fast-trackers tend to be more inflexible and rigid than most people, and they feel uncomfortable in spontaneous and unpredictable situations. Work makes them feel secure. It is the one thing they can control, or so they think, in an otherwise unwieldy life. Weekend lulls, when nothing is planned and the unexpected could happen, are traumatic for stress addicts.

A university professor said that she remembered leaving her office one Friday afternoon after a long, hard week. With butterflies in her stomach, she wondered what she would do during the weekend. At that point someone handed her an announcement that grant proposals were due in one month. Exhaling a huge sigh of relief, she knew she had something to carry her through another weekend, and calm descended over her. She was like an alcoholic, bottle under her arm, who was assured of plenty to drink:

> For me work was an anesthetic. It was tranquilizing. It numbed the pain, calmed me down, helped me forget and made me feel good. Folding that three-inch-thick computer printout under my arm made my adrenaline flow. That bundle was my security, promising to fill the hours and give me purpose, meaning and self-esteem. Knowing what I'd do that weekend, I was in full control. But after the proposal was written, the emptiness, unrest and depression returned.

▬ EXERCISE 4: HOW DO YOU EXERCISE CONTROL?

We all have a need to control at one time or other. This need can be expressed in a variety of ways: from the inability to delegate work to responsible employees to the refusal to compromise on choosing a restaurant. In the space following list some ways you exercise the need to control in your personal, professional and social life. After you have generated an exhaustive list, go back and put a check mark by each item you would like to change. State in concrete words what you will do to make these changes.

_____ 1. _____
        _____

_____ 2. _____
        _____

_____ 3. _____
        _____

_____ 4. _____
        _____

_____ 5. _____
        _____

_____ 6. _____
        _____

_____ 7. _____
        _____

_____ 8. _____
        _____

▬ EXERCISE 5: LETTING GO

Control comes in three forms: forcing, resisting and clinging.

Forcing is an *offensive* reaction in which we try to manipulate or impose our will on other people or situations.

Resisting is a *defensive* reaction in which we block the truth about other people or situations.

Clinging is an *avoidance* reaction in which we clutch the familiar and avoid change in favor of habit and routine.

Are you a forcer, resister or clinger? Think of as many things as you can that you have been forcing, resisting or clinging to in your own life. It may be resistance to a life change, refusal to accept someone's behavior or unwillingness to try something new. In the left-hand column list each aspect of your life that you are forcing, resisting or clinging to. In the right-hand column state what you can do to let go of and accept this part of your life over which you have no control.

Forcing			Acceptance
Resisting			Acceptance
Clinging			Acceptance

3. PERFECTIONISM

Preferring to do things myself rather than asking for help is part of my perfectionist syndrome. It's like that old phrase, "If you want it done right, do it yourself." If I do it, I know it's been done, I know it's been done completely and I know it's been done the way I want it done. If I had an employee I completely trusted to do it the way I would do it, I would give up the task. I'd like to find a support person who could do as complete a job as I would do. I haven't found one yet, although the people who work with me are very qualified and talented.

There is no pleasing the stress addict, no matter how hard you try. As perfectionists they complain about small things: "Why isn't the house clean?" or "Who left the cabinet door open?" or "Why isn't there any soap?" On the job, they are grumpy when little things are not exactly right. "You typed my name without my middle initial! You'll have to redo the whole letter," complains one compulsive worker. Another is concerned about more trivial things: "The door to the supply room should stay closed at all times!" Stress addicts are such sticklers that nothing can ever be perfect enough. They do not give either themselves or others permission to make mistakes. Making even the slightest error gives rise to self-recrimination. They hold high standards for themselves and judge others by those same inhuman principles.

An administrator shared his obsession for perfection:

To an extent I think I'm superhuman. I've always taken on more than I was capable of doing. It's not that I don't have the ability, but I just don't have the time. Physically, within a 24-hour period, I don't judge my time well enough and always take on more. I'm obsessed with creating lists by which I live, finding a way to fill in any extra spaces with obscure chores so that it will look as if I'm busy. By virtue of my lists, I cannot be content to accomplish something without laying the groundwork for something else. Fearing idleness, I have to be striving to accomplish some kind of goal or some block of work.

▬ EXERCISE 6: FROM "SHOULD" TO "COULD"

A big part of overcoming perfectionism is accepting things as they are. Overuse of the words "should," "ought" or "must" reflects our feeling that nothing we do is ever good enough.

This exercise is from Louise Hay. Think of at least three things that you "should" have done today or yesterday or last week. Write them down:

1. I should have _____

2. I should have _____
3. I should have _____

One man's "should list" looked like this:

1. "I should have finished that report on Friday."
2. "I should have taken more time to listen to her problem."
3. "I should have cleaned the house before company arrived."

Now look at how this man's perfectionism makes him feel shameful and guilty for his actions. If we asked him why he "should" have done those things, he would answer that his teachers always told him to finish what he started, his parents pounded into his brain that he should be sensitive to other people or that his culture taught him that "cleanliness is next to Godliness." "Shoulds" are shame-based, perfectionistic messages drilled into our minds at an early age. They are barriers to self-esteem.

You can turn those shame-based messages around by replacing the word "should" with "could."

1. "I *could* have finished that report on Friday."
2. "I *could* have taken more time to listen to her problem."
3. "I *could* have cleaned the house before company arrived."

Now look at *your* list of "shoulds." Substitute the word "could" for each of your "shoulds" and notice how it changes the meaning of the perfectionistic messages you send yourself.

1. I could have _____
2. I could have _____
3. I could have _____

The words you use to talk to yourself reinforce your perfectionism and feelings of shame and defeat. Changing those words can soften the blow and remind you that you always have a choice and that sometimes you may choose not to exercise certain choices.

— EXERCISE 7: GRATITUDE

Gratitude for the things we already have is another antidote to inhuman perfectionistic standards that make us feel as if we always fail. Accepting our mistakes with successes and taking the flaws with the shine release us from the bonds of self-defeating perfectionism.

Close your eyes and get comfortable. Take a deep breath and let your body relax. Inhale and exhale a few times. Think of as many things as you can that you are grateful for and that make your life worth living. Visualize what is precious in your life. See the things that you take for granted, things that would leave your life empty if you didn't have them. You can include material items, such as your car or house, as well as relationships with loved ones, such as a child, spouse, lover or pet. Let your thoughts come and visualize each one as vividly as you can. Acknowledge each important thought as it appears and feel the gratitude in your heart.

Write down the things in your life that you are grateful for in the space below. Practice this exercise regularly so that you begin to feel better about yourself and see how positive and rich your life already is.

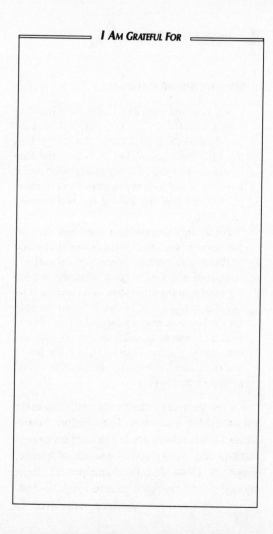

I AM GRATEFUL FOR

4. DIFFICULTY WITH RELATIONSHIPS

My husband complained about my working late at the office in the evening. So I bundled up all this stuff, took it home, closed myself in my bedroom and worked on it into the wee hours of morning. I'd fall asleep with work piled on top of me. My husband would come to bed and find his side of the bed covered with ledgers.

Finally he quit coming to bed and slept on the sofa. It was two years before I realized anything was wrong. When we separated, I wondered why I was crying about the bed being empty on the other side. I'd tell myself how dumb it was because he had been on the sofa for the last year anyway. I'd find myself almost falling off the bed, rolling over to try to find him there. I started purposely leaving books and stuff on his side of the bed, so there would be something there.

Excessive work interferes with intimate relationships and close friendships. Sometimes fast-trackers are dependent on others outside the workplace — usually a spouse, lover or close family member. All their thoughts and energies go into work, and little is left over for anything unrelated to work. As a result they often appear helpless with small things and lacking in common sense. One man was in his thirties before he knew the difference between lettuce and cabbage, and he was in his forties before he could tie a necktie. He was too busy working to take the time to understand the small things that get one through the day. Having someone else there to do them for him gave him more time to work. Learning to set a digital watch or to assemble a complicated children's toy can seem bothersome because it takes precious moments away from more important work tasks.

On his trip across Europe, Alvin left all decisions to his wife. She kept his wallet and passport. She managed their daily visits to museums, tours and various sites. She computed the change ratio from dollars to rubles and made the actual exchange. Alvin dutifully followed her lead.

Accomplished in their chosen fields, such people can be klutzy at home and in the social world because they have put all their energies into work. Imbalanced, they have few social skills and few interests outside of work. Either their topic of discussion is work or they remain silent during social conversations because their narrow scope of knowledge prevents them from participating.

Co-dependence on a loved one or friend strains relationships and causes resentments. The wife of a stress addict told me she resented the fact that her husband prided himself on his work but neglected their home life:

> The issue of control is a battle all the time. He's a perfectionist about his business. His condos are in such beautiful condition and look like model homes. If he gets a drop of paint anywhere it doesn't belong, he'll work hours to remove it. But our house is a dump if he has anything to do with it. He will not pick up after himself and he never cleans anything. Doing as little as he can, he doesn't even take out the garbage. If I ask him to help me with something he gets sullen and withdrawn.

Neglect of home and personal life is the biggest complaint spouses have. A housewife told me, "I'm tired of sloppy seconds. After my husband finishes working, there's nothing but cold leftovers for me and the kids." Spouses feel secondary, even jealous — and perhaps for good reason. They become suspicious that their mates are having an affair because of long and late work hours away from home. Even when no lovers are involved, spouses complain that there might as well be because the excessive work is just as hard to take.

The term "wedded to work" was coined for a good reason, and it knows no gender boundaries. A female architect confided that more than once she had mentally worked on a client's house plans during sexual intercourse with her husband. A gardener confessed that sometimes he, too, found himself designing landscapes while making love.

Stress addicts put more thought, time and energy into work than into intimate relationships with their families, socializing with friends, working on hobbies or enjoying leisure and recreational activities. They forget, ignore or minimize important family rituals and celebrations such as birthdays, reunions, anniversaries or holidays. They cannot stop long enough to fully participate because such events require total immersion of the person at the expense of losing endless hours of work.

Some stress addicts even use bargaining to get released from family "obligations."

They might tell a spouse, "I'll go to the family reunion with you next weekend, if you'll keep the kids out of my hair this weekend so that I can finish this sales report." Such promises of cutting down on work or spending more time with the family are frequently broken. As the weekend approaches, there's more work to be done, and the addict apologizes with, "Sorry, honey. Looks like you and the kids will have to go without me."

When strong-armed into going on family outings or leisure activities, work junkies do so dutifully but often begrudgingly. Their minds stay work-occupied almost all the way. They pull every trick in the book to work during the course of the outing: "I gotta go make a phone call" or "I'll just read this report while we wait for dinner."

EXERCISE 8: YOUR RELATIONSHIPS

Think of up to eight people who are important in your life: your spouse or love interest, co-workers, friends, parents, children or others. Put their names in the outer circles that encircle the "you" circle. Next draw a line symbolizing the nature of your relationship with each person. Straight lines stand for solid, healthy relationships. Jagged lines stand for bumpy or shaky relationships. Spirals stand for relationships you are confused or uncertain about.

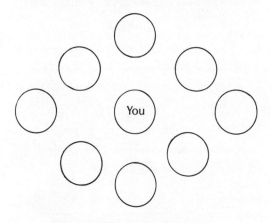

Exercise 8: Your Relationships

Solid Relationships = _____

Bumpy Relationships = ᘛᘚᘛᘚᘛᘚᘛᘚᘛᘚ

Uncertain Relationships = ℓℓℓℓℓℓℓℓ

After you have completed the exercise, answer the following questions:

1. What have you learned about your relationships? _____

_____

_____

2. What do you like about what you see?

_____

_____

_____

3. What do you dislike about what you see? _____

_____

_____

4. What could you change? _____

_____

_____

5. Do you want to change? _____

_____

_____

6. How would you do that? _____

_____

_____

7. Will you do it? _____

_____

_____

8. When will you begin? _____

_____

_____

— EXERCISE 9: STRENGTHENING RELATIONSHIPS

Think about your relationships and how they have suffered because of fast-track living. Complete the following sentences:

1. I can strengthen my family relationships by _____

_____

_____

2. I can strengthen my work relationships by _____

_____

_____

3. I can strengthen my social relationships by _____

_____

_____

4. I can strengthen my relationship with myself by _____

_____

_____

5. WORK BINGES

Stress addicts rarely work eight-hour days, five days a week. They are usually still plugging away after their co-workers have called it quits. The golden rule of the stress addicted is, "Do today what doesn't need doing until six months from now." They have trouble spreading their work over a period of time. They binge for days on a project until it is finished, rather than complete it in small segments of time.

Travis, a self-employed landscaper works day and night for three days until he completes a project, rather than spreading it out over a four- or five-day work week. Carol, a community college instructor, had the goal of completing all the work on her desk each day, no matter how long she had to stay at the office. The attitude of a healthy co-worker helped her rethink her compulsive attitude toward work: "There will always be plenty of work to do. No matter how hard and fast I work, I'll never really be able to catch up. So I just relax, take it easy and work steadily rather than try to stay ahead in this business."

Everybody has to overwork occasionally to meet deadlines. But when stress addicts binge on work, they often do it because of self-imposed early deadlines, not mandatory time frames. A report may not be due for six months, for example. But a work addict does a 12-hour marathon to complete it now, rather than complete it gradually over time. The concrete sense of completion is satisfying, and having the assignment out of the way early leaves time to focus on other work items. Sometimes their minds are not at rest until the project is completed, and they work day and night until it is done.

An office manager stress addict told me:

My supervisor needs a report by Friday, so I'd better have it done by Tuesday and typed by Wednesday. If I have changes to make or errors to fix, I can get them done and submit the report first thing on Friday, and he won't have to call me and ask for it. I self-impose deadlines all the time. Because I'm rarely late,

I usually give myself enough time to get where I'm going, even if it's across the street, with time to sit and read. If the meeting is at 1:00, I'll get there five minutes early. But I don't think anything's wrong with that. When I have projects that I have to submit to someone else, I work very hard so that I can get them done on time. The price I have to pay for procrastinating is unbearable. I go nuts. I panic. I can't sleep. I have such anxiety. Oh God! How will I get it done? Procrastination is a killer to me!

As the disease progresses, some addicts conceal work from family and friends, sneaking it when they get a chance. Work goes everywhere the addict goes: in briefcases or luggage, or for more serious addicts it goes under car seats, in glove compartments, in car trunks beneath spare tires, in dirty laundry bags or stuffed down inside pants and inside skirts. Some addicts work extra heavily after a quarrel or a major disappointment.

Kate's work obsession became her "weekend lover." She lied to her family so that she could rendezvous with work at the office:

I would tell my family that I was going shopping on a Saturday and I'd end up in my office working. Or I'd tell them I was going to my girlfriend's house. After calling my girlfriend's and not finding me, they'd call the office and say, "I thought you were going to Dottie's." I felt like I had been caught with my hand in the cookie jar.

— EXERCISE 10: WORK MODERATION

There are things you can do to change your habit of work binges. The goal is *work moderation:* keeping an even keel by abstaining from excessive *over*doing. For example, you may . . .

- Establish a more steady work schedule with regular hours, rather than working all the time or binging for weeks at a time.
- Set boundaries by confining your work hours to eight hours a day, five days a week or whatever boundaries best fit with your lifestyle and job type.
- Refrain from self-imposing strict, unrealistic deadlines and spread work activity out over a longer period of time.

MY GOALS FOR WORK MODERATION ARE . . .

1.

2.

3.

4.

5.

6.

— EXERCISE 11: WEEKLY WORK PLAN

Use this form to design a weekly work plan for yourself that helps you set boundaries for one week.

Monday:

Tuesday:

Wednesday:

Thursday:

Friday:

Saturday:

Sunday:

When the week is over, ask yourself the following questions:

1. **What things need changing for the next week?** _____
_____
_____
_____

2. **What part of the plan worked well enough for me to keep on an ongoing basis?** _____
_____
_____
_____

3. **Additional comments or ideas:** _____
_____
_____
_____

6. DIFFICULTY RELAXING AND HAVING FUN

I always try to relax, but I don't relax very well. Sometimes when I'm exhibiting compulsive behaviors, I'll tell myself, "Why don't you just stop and enjoy the moment? Live for the moment. Try it!" And I don't know what that means. I'm always in fast forward. Maybe I think I would be bored.

Restlessness is the hallmark of stress addiction. Why can't stress addicts just relax and enjoy themselves? It sounds so simple, but it's not. The "Just Say No" campaign is useless with stress addicts. Turning down work or cutting back on hours is like asking a heroin addict to refuse that next fix, the alcoholic to turn down that drink or a compulsive eater to forego that second piece of chocolate cake. It's just not that easy.

Many stress addicts report hearing a nagging voice in their heads when they try to relax or unwind. This is their disease speaking. The voice tells them that what they are doing is totally unproductive and a complete waste of time. "You will have nothing to show for this waste of time!" They start to feel guilty because they are taking it easy. It doesn't feel right. Becoming restless and even shaky, they start feeling useless and bad about themselves. They may even fool themselves that it is not their nature to sit still for very long. The guilt usually wins the battle when the addicted are not in recovery. They end up "white knuckling it" until they can get themselves out of the social situation and back into busy pursuits. Work preoccupied, they take themselves too seriously, seldom laugh or smile and have difficulty having fun.

The spouse of a stress addict described her husband's inability to let go and enjoy himself:

> It's really difficult to pull him away from any of his work activities. He gets really anxious when he's not working, and then I feel guilty if I try to get him to do something with me other than work. I wind up feeling as if I have deprived him of something.

▬ EXERCISE 12: WHAT HELPS YOU RELAX?

There are many ways to unwind, relax and have fun: stress-relief exercises, mind-relaxation techniques, physical exercise, yoga, meditation, prayer, massage, daily inspirational readings or hobbies.

Think of three things you like to do the most that are fun and help you relax. Write them down in the blanks below. Now think of the last time you did each one. Was it a day ago, a week ago, a month ago or years ago? Beneath each favorite thing, put how long it's been since you've done it. What does this information tell you about how you're living your life? Did you have trouble even thinking of three favorite things? Are you doing the things you want to do in your life? Or are you living your life for someone else? What enjoyable pastime can you plan for yourself?

1. **First favorite thing:** _____

   _____

   Last time I did it: _____

   _____

2. **Second favorite thing:** _____

   _____

   Last time I did it: _____

   _____

3. **Third favorite thing:** _____

   _____

   Last time I did it: _____

   _____

What does this tell me about how I'm living my life? _____

_____

_____

What goals for relaxing and having fun can I set for myself? _____

_____

_____

■ EXERCISE 13: LEARNING TO PLAY

Sometimes fast-trackers must rediscover how to have fun. We can do this by getting in touch with our playful inner child. Visualize the little boy or little girl inside yourself. What fun things did your inner child want to do in childhood that he or she never got a chance to do? _____

_____

_____

How did missing out on these opportunities make your inner child feel? _____

_____

_____

It's never too late to get in touch with our playful child — whether we walk barefoot in a rainstorm, go skating or build sandcastles in the sand. Think of as many playful things you can that will release your inner child. Then do them. Don't let your self-consciousness or fear of being silly stand in the way.

After you've done the things you've always wanted to do, how do you feel? _____

_____

_____

7. BROWNOUTS

A car swerves down the highway. The man behind the wheel is high but not from booze. He's high from work. The man is a minister who is writing his Sunday morning sermon as he zips down the interstate. You've seen them before: motorists trying to read the newspaper, talking on the telephone or eating their lunch as they speed to get somewhere. When behind the wheel of a car, some fast-trackers actually put their own lives and those of other passengers in danger.

The stress-addicted suffer from something I call *brownouts*, in which they have memory losses of long conversations or trips to and from a destination because of mental preoccupation with planning and work. Brownouts are also a side effect of tuning out the here and now. Having lived in an addicted family all their lives, adult children learn that the "now" is scary, unpredictable and uncomfortable. Stress addicts live in the future because of their undeveloped ability to live in the present.

Different from the fantasies of daydreams, brownouts result from stress and burn-out. One man told me:

> My wife sometimes tells me she thinks I have Alzheimer's disease. But it's just that my mind is on my work and nothing else is important at that particular moment. I'll ask her a question. And rather than wait for an answer, my mind has already jumped to something else. I'll ask the question again, and she'll say, "Do you realize you've asked me that three times?" And I don't remember asking the question, much less receiving an answer.

A woman stress addict admitted her staff said she has a hearing problem:

They would say things to me while I'd be working on something. They'd be telling me about a concern and I wouldn't hear them. Because something else had my attention, I'd tune out everything around me. Many times I'll be driving somewhere else and end up at the office. Because my mind is on five million other things, I get in my car and put on the automatic pilot without thinking.

A university professor also experiences brownouts while driving. She frequently finds herself in the middle of downtown, forgetting her destination. Her mind has been thinking about a problem at work or planning a special project. Once while driving, she had been mentally trying to coordinate faculty course assignments for the next three academic terms. Suddenly she found herself pulling into the parking lot of a condominium where she had not lived for many years, and she didn't even remember driving there.

Another woman told me that while she was in bed, she'd try to figure out how to solve a problem at work. Once, feeling thirsty, she went to the kitchen to get a glass of water. With her mind still on the problem, she returned to bed. Fifteen minutes later she heard the sound of running water. She realized that in her stupor she had put her glass under the spigot, turned the water on and walked away without turning the water off.

Associates, friends and family members will often complain that fast-trackers ask the same question two or three times. If the question they ask requires a lengthy response, their minds jump to another thought without waiting to process the answer. Or they are involved in so many things at once, they do not even realize they have already asked the question.

One man spent a week's vacation with his family in Florida. One day, after working on a sales report, he realized his wallet was missing. He had the whole family in an uproar searching for the lost wallet. They spent hours turning the house upside down, emptying bags of rotting garbage, opening drawers and searching under beds. He even accused the housekeeper of moving it when she was cleaning. They retraced his steps for 10 miles by car, trekking in and out of stores, asking clerks and looking on top of drink counters in the convenience store. Later in the evening he found the wallet right where he had put it, in a side pocket of his briefcase.

Fast-trackers spend a lot of time mentally planning and thinking about future events. Although present in body, their minds are often working while eating and driving, carrying on lengthy conversations or sometimes even during sexual activity. They have repeated episodes of forgetfulness because their minds are on completing the job, rather than concentrating on the present moment. While healthy people pay attention to whom they speak, where they put things and what they are doing at the moment, stress addicts don't want to fool with taking the time to worry with those "unimportant" things that take a back seat to the work at hand.

Her husband's forgetfulness became a source of grave concern for the wife of this stress addict:

> He's very forgetful. In fact, because I thought he might have brain damage, I started worrying about him. He forgets where he puts important things like the cordless phone. He's always walking around the house with it, then misplacing it. Keys, checkbooks, bills and

any items not nailed down get lost. But he never loses his work stuff. He knows exactly where it is. That's saying a lot because his office at home is really a mess. But he loses everything else.

— EXERCISE 14: LIVING IN THE NOW

You can combat brownouts by learning to live in the now. Begin living for today and resist your mind's attempts to preoccupy you with yesterday, tomorrow or next week. You can achieve this by paying attention to the people you are with at the moment, focusing on the present and working on your relationships by putting time and energy into them. Try the Living In The Now technique:

The next time you go to work, pretend you have entered the workplace for the very first time. Look at the people and places around you as if you are seeing and appreciating them for the first time. Notice what hangs on the walls, smell the flowers on someone's desk, see the color of a blouse or jacket a colleague is wearing, pay attention to the colors of the floor or the architecture of the buildings on the same street. Be mindful of the eyes of a co-worker, subordinate or boss. Look into their eyes and see their humanity.

When you try this technique, you will discover another world, which has always been open to you, but which you have never seen before because of your fast-paced lifestyle.

Now write down your thoughts and feelings of the experience in the space provided below:

_____

_____

_____

_____

_____

■ EXERCISE 15: BROWNOUT STRESS PROFILE

Brownouts often result from stress and burnout. If you are on the fast track, you are at risk for physical, mental, emotional and social stress. The Brownout Stress Profile* can help you identify where your stress comes from and help you eliminate brownouts.

_____

*Source: Bryan Robinson, Bobbie Rowland, and Mick Coleman, (1989). *Home-Alone Kids* (Lexington, MA: Lexington Books, 1989). Used with permission.

Brownout Stress Profile*

Place a "1" in the space beside each symptom that you have noticed in yourself during the past month.

Physical Stress

___ Headaches	___ Teeth grinding
___ Fatigue	___ Insomnia
___ Weight change	___ Restlessness
___ Colds or allergies	___ Accident-prone
___ Pounding heart	___ Upset stomach
___ Tension in muscles of neck or shoulders	___ Increased alcohol, drug or tobacco use

Total Physical ___ Stress Score	*Add your scores. Write your score in the space to the left.*

Mental Stress

___ Forgetfulness	___ Errors in judgment
___ Dulling of the senses	___ Confusion at home
___ Decline in problem-solving skills	___ Poor concentration
	___ Loss of creativity
___ Lowered productivity	___ Boredom
	___ Mental exhaustion
___ Negative attitude	___ Confusion at work

Total Mental ___ Stress Score	*Add your scores. Write your score in the space to the left.*

Emotional Stress

__ Anxiety	__ Irritability
__ Feeling "uptight"	__ Depression
__ Mood swings	__ Nervous laughter
__ Constant worrying	__ Self-criticism
__ Bad temper	__ Crying spells
__ Loss of interest in hobbies	__ Easily discouraged

Total Emotional __ Stress Score	*Add your scores. Write your score in the space to the left.*

Social Stress

__ Isolation	__ Lashing out at co-workers
__ Resentment of others	__ Nagging others
__ Loneliness	__ Being impatient
__ Lashing out at family	__ Clamming up
__ Lashing out at friends	__ Using people
__ Lowered sex drive	__ Being vindictive

Total Social __ Stress Score	*Add your scores. Write your score in the space to the left.*

Scoring: Because we are unique, we have different levels of stress and different kinds of stress symptoms. To determine how much *physical, mental, emotional* and *social* stress you have, follow these steps:

1. Write your *physical, mental, emotional* and *social* stress scores in the blanks on the grid below.
2. Put an "X" on the line above each stress symptom that matches your score. For example, if your *physical* stress score is six, then put an X on the vertical line that is across from the number six.
3. Repeat step 2 for your *mental, emotional* and *social* stress scores.

Interpretation:

Review your stress scores on the grid. What stress symptoms are most common? Compare your scores to those of your family members. Plan a family meeting to discuss the different levels of stress within your family. Consider the reasons for the stress found in your family and think of ways to reduce it. Most regions of the country offer stress-reducing classes through local community colleges and universities, mental health centers, churches and county cooperative extension offices.

Brownout Stress Grid

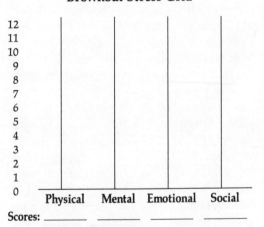

	Physical	Mental	Emotional	Social
12				
11				
10				
9				
8				
7				
6				
5				
4				
3				
2				
1				
0				

Scores: _____ _____ _____ _____

8. IMPATIENCE AND IRRITABILITY

I have angrily left carts of groceries at supermarkets because they didn't have enough check-out people. Then I had to go shop again later. I don't tell people off or create a scene, line jump or stand there and stomp. But I'll make a conscious decision that the line is too long for me and these things are not worth the wait. I always have to be somewhere because I put myself on such a tight schedule.

Time is the most precious commodity of fast-trackers. They do not like to be kept waiting. They are easily annoyed and cannot tolerate delays in grocery, restaurant, movie lines or waiting in doctors' offices. Many stress addicts are deliberately late or get routines down to a science so they won't have to wait.

A salesman who lives in Atlanta and has sales territory in Alabama told me how he times to the minute the trip from his house to the airport to prevent waiting. He leaves his house an hour before flight time. It takes 30 to 45 minutes for him to get there, and 10 to 15 minutes to park his car and check his bags. With this system he can walk up and be the last person on board because he "hates sitting and waiting for things." Instead of leaving an hour earlier to prevent stressful hurrying, he says there are too many other things to accomplish in the extra hour that he cannot afford to give up. So he takes his chances that he will not get tied up in traffic and that the plane will take off on time.

Another corporate supervisor told me that she deliberately developed a pattern of being late so that instead of waiting for someone, she could use that time to cram in more work:

> I'm always late. There have been so many times in my life when I've been on time and had to wait for people. In order to be on time, I had to stop something else that was important. I started consciously deciding to go five minutes late because I figured my appointment wouldn't be ready for me anyway. My first day on this job, I made it a point to be on time and ended up waiting for 10 minutes. I don't think I was ever on time again in six years.

More long-term waiting, such as waiting for someone to return a much-sought-after book to the library, can also unleash impatience and irritability. I realized I needed help the day I jumped down the librarian's throat about a book that had been checked out by a faculty member for the remainder of the term. On my second special trip to the library just to get this book, I was furious when told it was still unavailable. I demanded that she search the computer and tell me the person's name so that I could talk with him. She searched the name and gave me a strange look. "We're not supposed to give out that information, but in this case I think it's okay."

"Well?" I demanded impatiently.

"It says *you* have the book already checked out, sir."

Needless to say, I was speechless and embarrassed beyond belief. The book had been in my possession for six months in a huge stack of other books in my office, and I didn't even know it. Somehow waiting was always easier after that.

Some short-tempered stress addicts become enraged over a minor disagreement. In their impatience they often interrupt others in mid-sentence to respond to questions or concerns that have not been fully verbalized. But if *they* are interrupted while in the middle of work, it's a different story. Nothing will raise the work addict's ire as much as an interruption. They even get irritable and depressed after a day or two being forced to live without work.

Irritability and impatience are not always vented through full-blown anger. The wife of a stress addict described how her husband sometimes expresses hostility through passive-aggression:

> He has a lot of passive-aggressive behaviors. His anger is indirect. He doesn't admit to being annoyed but instead acts sullen, with a facial expression that looks troubled. But if I ask him if he's bothered, he says no. Then he'll do something spiteful not very long after — something he knows upsets me — and then deny having done it to manipulate me.

When impatience leads to impulsiveness, nowhere is the adage "haste makes waste" more appropriate. Important decisions are made and projects launched before all facts are gathered, before all options are thoroughly explored or before all phases have been finalized. Results can be disastrous when the addiction outruns careful thought and reflection.

Kate gained a reputation at her job for taking something, going with it and then going back and cleaning up her tracks:

> I do that all the time. An idea will come to me and I'll say, "Ah! This is great!" And I'll jump in and go with it. I'll have it moving and

be way ahead of everyone else. They're sitting back and taking it all apart and thinking through everything, and I'm way ahead of them. It took us two years to clean up the billing mess. Our billing procedures were behind because we were working so far ahead of ourselves. But I get high off it. "Why not make it happen, then we can go back and fix it," was the way I thought about it. We have to keep the ball in the air or it'll die. If you let it go back to committee 15 different times, you've lost your spark and it's not the same.

**— EXERCISE 16: THE PATIENCE = IMPATIENCE
THERMOMETER**

On the Patience-Impatience Thermometer below, color in red how much patience
you ordinarily have. Then use another color
to show how much patience you would like
to have.

— 120	**Patience**
— 110	
— 100	
— 90	
— 80	
— 70	
— 60	
— 50	
— 40	
— 30	
— 20	
— 10	
— -10	
— -20	**Impatience**

What can you do to develop more patience? _____

_____

_____

_____

━━ EXERCISE 17: SELF-AFFIRMATIONS

Writing down self-affirmations helps them to become a part of you. In the blanks below write your own affirmations about developing patience. You can also use my examples, writing them verbatim or rewriting them in your own words:

- *I am a patient and thoughtful person.*
- *I am worth all the time in the world.*
- *Today I am patient and confident in my personal growth.*
- *Today there is no haste, rush or hurry because patience is my sidekick.*
- *Waiting is a natural part of life that I wear like a loose garment.*
- *The slogans "One step at a time" and "Easy does it" remind me to be patient in my daily life.*

1. _____
2. _____
3. _____
4. _____
5. _____
6. _____
7. _____
8. _____
9. _____
10. _____

9. SELF-INADEQUACY

I like to see progress. Of course, being in the people business and the education business, that's almost a contradiction in terms. You cannot be concrete when you're working with people. You have to be abstract. But there are other aspects of my job that allow me to see immediate progress. If I work really hard on a report, a letter or some type of document, it always looks better when it's completed. I like to see the finished product. It has to do with the way I present myself as a manager to my supervisor, to my peers, to the people I supervise and to my colleagues in the community. I think a lot of that stems from the syndrome I grew up with: Be a good girl, do the right thing, follow the rules, do it right, make sure it's perfect, make straight As, do the best you can, it better be good, make it look good and see the results. I'm very result oriented, which is definitely tied in with approval from the world and myself. I used to say that I didn't care what people thought about me, but I really do.

The stress addict's sense of inadequacy and poor self-esteem lead to a strong emphasis on production. Compulsive workers must see the concrete results of what they do. They are often more interested in the final result of work than in the process. Said one, "The only time I felt good about myself was when I was producing 'things' so that I could constantly prove that I was okay." Despite repeated accomplishments, addicted workers continue to feel badly about themselves. Work gives them a temporary high and a feeling of self-worth. But one achievement after another is never enough. They are like alcoholics who drink to feel better, except they substitute work for booze. They continue to push themselves harder and harder, thinking that eventually they will gain self-esteem and be able to stop or at least slow down.

Aside from maintaining control, there are other reasons that the work addicted are unable to ask for help. One woman told me that she believes her husband's inability to ask for help is also tied to self-esteem: "He never asks for help. If he were dying in the middle of the street, couldn't walk and a million people passed by him, he wouldn't ask one of them for help. To me it seems as if he won't ask for help because he doesn't think he's worth helping."

— EXERCISE 18: POSITIVE AND NEGATIVE

Use a watch or clock that counts seconds to time yourself on this exercise. List five positive traits about yourself that you can describe in one word:

1. _____

2. _____

3. _____

4. _____

5. _____

How long did it take? _____.

Now list five negative traits about yourself that you can describe in one word.

1. _____

2. _____

3. _____

4. _____

5. _____

How long did it take? _____.

Compare the time it took to list the positive traits with the time it took to list the negative ones. Almost always it is quicker to name five negative things than five positive things because the negative is what fast-trackers focus on the most. When you can find the positive side of yourself as quickly as you can find the negative, you will know that balance and serenity are coming into your life. Try this exercise from time to time as you work on positive feelings toward yourself and see what changes occur in the lapsed times.

— EXERCISE 19: TRANSFORMING NEGATIVE MESSAGES

During the next week, be on the lookout for negative conversations you have with yourself. Keep track of these negative statements by writing them down without censorship in the daily log on page 71. At the end of the week, look over your list. Star the ones that occur more than once. You may be surprised at how often you tell yourself how "stupid" or how "unworthy" you are. These are the unhealthy messages that you live by. They govern your feelings, thoughts and behaviors. They tell you what you think of yourself, reflect how you behave and even may indicate how others perceive you.

Beside every negative thought you listed for the week, substitute a positive affirmation. Affirmations are positive declarations that help us recognize our true inner worth. Examples are:

"I can stand on my own two feet."
"I am already good enough just as I am."
"I am deserving of the best life has to offer."

Work first with the messages that you most often send yourself. Practice sending the positive affirmations to yourself as often as you can during the day . . . in the morning as you look in the mirror, on the way to work, while waiting in a line or before falling asleep at night. Practicing positive affirmations makes you feel more positive about yourself.

DAILY LOG

Monday:

Tuesday:

Wednesday:

Thursday:

Friday:

Saturday:

Sunday:

— EXERCISE 20: MORE SELF-AFFIRMATIONS

As further practice on self-affirmations, complete the following sentences:

—— *THINGS ABOUT ME THAT I LIKE ARE . . .* ——

SOME POSITIVE AFFIRMATIONS ABOUT ME ARE . . .

10. SELF-NEGLECT

I don't feel productive unless I'm working. When I get depressed, I get immobilized and paralyzed, just can't do anything and feel helpless. At work you can't say, "I didn't sleep last night or I can't work today, I'm depressed." I've always had an insomnia problem, and there have been many times when I've gone three or four nights without sleep, but I still have to go to work. It makes me cranky, uncomfortable and grouchy, but nobody's going to say, "You don't have to go into work today; you stay home and sleep." That's not the way the world works.

Overwork leads to self-neglect, a host of psychosomatic complaints and physical health problems. Stress addicts tend to ignore their own needs. They neglect their physical (nutrition, rest and exercise) and mental (play and recreation) health. Those who work in sedentary jobs are especially at risk. They may not get enough exercise, particularly if they work binge for 12 or 15 hours a day. Poor nutrition comes from grabbing fast foods so that they can work through lunch or skip lunch altogether. Accompanying addictions, such as chain smoking, caffeine habits and occasionally alcohol consumption, contribute to health demise. Constant stress that addicts impose on themselves from lack of recreation, overcommitment, lack of sleep and overworking also lead to health problems.

Fast-trackers tend to ignore anything that distracts them from work, including warning signs of physical illness. When symptoms of health problems do appear, stress addicts are more likely than most people to let them go unattended, to deny their presence or to minimize their importance. They put work before everything else, even medical needs. They ignore aches and pains that could be telling them their body is tired or even in danger. Although a part of the addict's mind is aware of the problem, another part doesn't want to take the time to stop and think about it, let alone have it checked. Left unattended, these health hazards could ultimately cost them their lives.

The stress addiction of an insurance company supervisor caused her many health problems, but her story has a happy ending:

I always had allergies and headache problems. Two years ago I developed this devastating stomach pain with irritation and indigestion. I took the whole gamut of tests, and there was nothing there except damage to the lower end of the esophagus from gastric juice. My stomach hasn't hurt since I started walking in the evenings two months ago. That's made a significant difference for my stress management. I understand myself better and see what happened to me. I used to drink coffee all day long, but now I only drink one-and-a-half cups a day.

■ EXERCISE 21: SELF-PORTRAITS

Using crayons or colored pens, draw a picture of how you look when you suffer self-neglect. Your merit as an artist doesn't count.

In the space below draw another picture of yourself showing how you look when you take care of yourself.

What do the two drawings tell you? What is different about them? What colors are dominant? Which drawing makes you feel better? Why?

▬ EXERCISE 22: ALL THE NEWS ABOUT YOU

On a separate sheet of paper write several newspaper headlines that illustrate how life on the fast track has caused you to neglect your physical, emotional, social and spiritual needs. Underneath each headline write a "newspaper" sentence or two on how you will pay attention to this neglect.

Here's an example:

> "SPIRITUAL NEEDS IN SMITH HOUSE-HOLD ONLY SCRATCH THE SURFACE"
>
> Ed Smith has neglected his inner needs because of his life in the fast lane. He tried a good night's rest, a week by the seashore, a two-mile hike and a healthy meal but they only scratched the surface. To get to the crux of the problem Smith is looking deeper into himself. Through meditation, prayer and inspirational daily readings, he vows to confront and resolve his compulsive need for fast-track living.

2. BALANCE AND SERENITY FROM FAST-TRACK LIVING

The natural inclination is to approach recovery from fast-track living in a hurried way — to cram it into your schedule and rush through it. Such an approach is self-defeating because recovery cannot be rushed. There is no such thing as a "quick fix." Recovery from fast-track living is a gradual process that takes commitment and time. Give yourself plenty of time for recovery to occur and give yourself credit for the small gains you make. Don't focus on all that needs to be done. Instead pat yourself on the back for the baby steps you make along the way. This is an important reminder so that you won't become frustrated and sabotage your healing process. You will not see the immediate concrete product that you are accustomed to. But if you stay with it, you will begin to see results.

Achieving and maintaining balance is the goal of those who want to develop their full potential. Fast-trackers are thrown off balance because of the neglect of other areas in their lives. If you want to move forward on the road of recovery, your wheels have to be balanced. We function as harmonious and whole human beings when balance occurs in four major areas of life:

> self
> family
> play
> healthy work

The self area includes attending to such personal needs as self-esteem, spiritual nurturance, nutrition and physical exercise.

Family includes positive communication and communion with loved ones. Today's society has many family configurations, and "family" means many different things to different people. Your family can be a spouse; it can include both a spouse and children; it can include unmarried lovers who cohabitate or adults who reside with older parents or siblings.

The play arena extends our needs for social relationships with others outside the family.

Healthy work habits include being effective and productive on the job, enjoying what we do for a living, working moderately and giving equal time to other areas of our lives.

Achieving this balance is sometimes a tightwire act. One way to view your life is to imagine it as a wheel made up of four spokes: *healthy work, family, play* and *self*. Each spoke is valued equally and gets equal attention if your wheel is to keep its shape. When one quadrant is unattended, the circle starts to deflate, loses its shape, and becomes unbalanced and lopsided. Nobody is perfectly balanced. But the closer you come, the fuller, more centered and more alive you feel as a human being. And you will become a more self-contented person all the way *around*.

Taking time to develop a balance among all four areas of your life wheel will ensure more harmony within yourself, at home, at work and at play. The following inventory will help you find the area in which balance is lacking. Knowledge of where imbalance occurs will help you develop a self-care plan.

━ EXERCISE 23: LIFE INVENTORY

There are four areas to this life inventory: **healthy work, family, play** and **self.**

1 = Never True
2 = Sometimes True
3 = Often True
4 = Always True

Put the number that best fits you in the blank beside each statement. At the end of each area you will get your total score by adding the eight numbers in each area and putting the sum in the blank at the end of the area.

Area 1: Healthy Work

____ 1. I have many interests outside my work duties.

____ 2. I spend as much time after hours with family and friends as I do with co-workers.

____ 3. I enjoy my work today as much as ever, and I am productive and effective at what I do.

____ 4. I work overtime only on special occasions.

____ 5. I am able to leave my work at the workplace.

____ 6. I am good at organizing and pacing my work time so that it doesn't interfere with other commitments.

____ 7. I work moderately, pace myself and confine my job to regular working hours.

____ 8. I spend an equal amount of time relaxing and socializing with friends as I do working.

____ **Total Work Score**

Area 2: Family

___ 1. I communicate well with the members of my family.

___ 2. I take an active interest in the lives of my other family members.

___ 3. My family spends quality time together.

___ 4. My family plays together and takes family outings regularly.

___ 5. I participate actively in family celebrations and traditions.

___ 6. I have good interpersonal relationships with other family members.

___ 7. I enjoy spending time with my family.

___ 8. My family and work life are in harmony with each other.

___ **Total Family Score**

Area 3: Play

____ 1. I socialize with friends who are not co-workers.

____ 2. I enjoy social gatherings.

____ 3. I like to unwind with friends.

____ 4. I go out socially with friends.

____ 5. My social life and work life are in harmony with each other.

____ 6. I enjoy inviting friends to my house for dinner.

____ 7. I like to play and have fun with others.

____ 8. It feels good to laugh, have a fun time and get my mind off work.

____ **Total Play Score**

Area 4: Self

_____ 1. I plan time each day just for me to do whatever I want to do.

_____ 2. For fun I have a hobby or recreation that I enjoy.

_____ 3. I take time out each week for my spiritual development, either church or synagogue, inspirational readings, meditation or a 12-Step program.

_____ 4. I eat nutritional, well balanced meals.

_____ 5. I make sure I get adequate rest.

_____ 6. I take physical exercise daily.

_____ 7. I send myself positive mental messages and try to look for the best in myself.

_____ 8. I make sure I get my personal needs met.

_____ **Total Self Score**

Scoring: Using the Balance Wheel of Life that follows, put an "X" on the number in each area that corresponds with your total score. Draw a line from that number to the

center of the wheel. Then darken the entire
area of the circle from your total score back
to the number "8." For example, if your **total
self score** is 16, put an X over the number 16
in the **self** area of the wheel. Draw a line
from 16 to the center of the circle; darken
that area from the center outward, and between 8 and 16. Repeat these steps for all
four areas of the wheel. The part of the
wheel that has the biggest shaded area is the
area in which you are most balanced. The
part that is less complete is the area of your
life that needs attention.

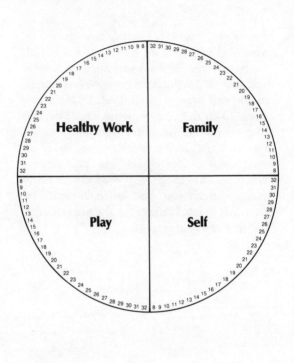

— EXERCISE 24: SELF-CARE PLAN

Based on your Balance Wheel of Life, develop a self-care plan in the work, family,
play and self areas of your life. For each area
set goals that will help you achieve greater
balance and serenity in your life.

SELF-CARE PLAN

Work:

Family:

Play:

Self:

> *You are looking at the
> only person in the world who can
> determine your happiness.*

I challenge you to affirm and love your-self. Be yourself. Pamper yourself. Forgive and care for yourself. Enjoy your own com-pany and be your own best friend. Do the things for you that you would do for the ones you love the most. And you will heal.

Other Books by Bryan E. Robinson, Ph.D.

Heal Your Self-Esteem
Recovery From Addictive Thinking
ISBN 1-55874-119-4 .... $9.95

Work Addiction
Hidden Legacies of Adult Children
ISBN 1-55874-023-6 .... $8.95

Soothing Moments
Daily Meditations For Fast-Track Living
ISBN 1-55874-075-9 .... $6.95

Am I Addicted To Work?
Code 2154   (Pamphlet) .... .95

Health Communications, Inc.
3201 S.W. 15th Street
Deerfield Beach, Florida 33442-8190
Or call (800) 851-9100 or FAX (305) 360-0034